Best Quotes About Life

365

Motivational Sayings to Inspire You to Be Successful

Inhale, Exhale and Repeat After Me!

Nicola Goldman

Dedication

I dedicate this book
to all
My teachers,
Past and future

Table of Contents

INTRODUCTION 7

HOW TO USE THIS BOOK 10

IMPORTANT THINGS TO NOTE 12

365 BEST QUOTES ABOUT LIFE 13

Introduction

It is no myth that words have power. It's almost baffling how a carefully selected group of words have the ability to influence one's life and decisions. A set of words should be able to influence your life positively for it to be termed as inspirational. It is safe to say that we all need a bit of inspiration in life. Some of us more than others, but a quote a day can go a long way in shaping one's destiny.

The goal of this book is to give the reader a good start to any day. It contains the very best of inspirational quotes, carefully selected to give you that extra boost you need every day. Not only do you get that inspirational quote in this book, but you will also get to learn the in-depth meaning of each quote and how you can relate to it.

We often look for inspiration in all the wrong places; yet, inspiration lies within us. In this book, you will discover the potential that lies within you. You will finally understand how you are your *own* motivation. You will develop courage to face every challenge that comes your way.

Truly understanding one's self is the beginning of realizing potential. Once you realize your potential, it will be difficult for anything to hold you back.

These quotes encourage you to see the greatness that is within you and guide you in unlocking your potential.

Reading this book is a journey of self-discovery. In this journey, you will be able to comprehend how to influence those around you to recognize the internal motivation they need.

This book is for everyone, regardless of age, gender, career, position, or any other aspect of life.

Self-discovery is optional. Not many seek it, but we all need it. When you picture all the things you could achieve upon finding your true purpose in life, you will find that self-discovery is an inevitable journey for us all. The words of this book are just the initial stepping stones of your journey.

For a leader or anyone tasked with a presentation of any kind, this book can come in handy in all stages of your presentation. Starting from preparation, to rehearsal, and finally on stage, you will be able to meaningfully connect with your audience and bring them to an understanding of your material.

If you are a boss, you probably know that your team looks up to you for guidance. Now picture yourself being an inspirational boss so that, whenever you talk, your crew feels so motivated that they produce results beyond your

expectations. Use the inspiration you receive from this book and gift it to others.

I am so certain you will find this book uplifting that you will find yourself giving this book as a gift to all the important people in your life. Since the pages contain quotes for each day of the year, they will never run out of inspirational quotes. Inspiration is a timeless gift one can use for a lifetime.

How to use this book

The inspirational quotes in this book have a specific purpose for your life; therefore, it is imperative that you make it a point to read at least one quote each day. All provided quotes have different impacts. There is always a quote that directly relates to your current situation.

Below is a simple guide on how to utilize this book to its full potential:

1. **Maximize the book's content**

This simply means that you ensure you have read each of the quotes within the book. This does not mean that one reads the whole book in one day.

For maximum utility of this book, you can decide to either be reading one quote a day or a few quotes a day. In so doing, the effectiveness of the quotes will definitely be visible in your life.

2. **Be inspired daily**

The capacity of quality inspirational quotes in this book is enough to cover a whole year and more than a third of the second year if used daily.

Make it a daily routine that you infuse your mornings with at least one inspirational quote. It does not have to be in the order they are written; you may select a random quote and use it to get the inspiration that you need each day.

3. **Consistency is key**

We all desire long term results as the effects are long lasting. For you to get long term results, you will have to be disciplined enough that no morning goes by without you reading a quote from this book.

Adopt it as a lifestyle and live it like you mean it. The eventual results are effective no matter your position or lifestyle.

4. **Relate**

Having the ability to relate the passages within is a very important aspect of reading this book. You should take your time and internalize each quote. Afterwards, you should be able to identify how each quote fits into your current situation, or your life in general. Finding the point of connection between the quote and your life is the best way to get the most out of the inspiration offered.

5. **Challenge yourself**

Some quotes in this book are aimed at ensuring that you soar to new heights and attain what are deemed to be unreachable goals. Once you get to such a quote, the ideal way to go about it is to challenge yourself by breaking the bigger target into smaller, manageable targets; after all,

it is better to try and fail than fail to try.

Important things to note

It is important that the reader understands that the quotes contained in this book have original authors and as such, are not the works of the author of this book. The author of this book provides guidance to the reader in regards to the selected quotes that appear in this book.

Every quote written in this book is applicable to all regardless of the gender, age, or any other factor indicated on any given quote. The reader should not dismiss any quote on the grounds of gender sensitivity, age restriction, social status, etc.

While sharing any quote from this book, please refer to the original author provided and not to the author of this book.

The reader should note that some quotes hold a deeper meaning rather than the surface meaning:

" I can't change the direction of the wind, but I can adjust my sails to always reach my destination."

Always remember to ruminate and internalize the deepest possible meaning of every quote. This will maximize your inspiration and move you to action.

365 Best Quotes About Life

Your time is limited, so don't waste it living someone else's life. Don't be trapped by dogma – which is living with the results of other people's thinking.

– Steve Jobs -

The purpose of our lives is to be happy.

– Dalai Lama -

Get busy living or get busy dying.

– Stephen King -

Never let the fear of striking out keep you from playing the game.

– Babe Ruth -

Many of life's failures are people who did not realize how close they were to success when they gave up.

– Thomas A. Edison -

If you want to live a happy life, tie it to a goal, not to people or things.

– Albert Einstein -

Do all the good you can, for all the people you can, in all the ways you can, as long as you can.

– Hillary Clinton -

Turn your wounds into wisdom.

– Oprah Winfrey -

Not how long, but how well you have lived is the main thing.

– Seneca -

Money and success don't change people; they merely amplify what is already there.

– Will Smith -

If life were predictable it would cease to be life, and be without flavor.

– Eleanor Roosevelt -

The whole secret of a successful life is to find out what is one's destiny to do, and then do it.

– Henry Ford -

You only live once, but if you do it right, once is enough.

– Mae West -

The big lesson in life, baby, is never be scared of anyone or anything.

– Frank Sinatra -

Sing like no one's listening, love like you've never been hurt, dance like nobody's watching, and live like its heaven on earth.

– Attributed to various sources -

Life is not a problem to be solved, but a reality to be experienced.

– Soren Kierkegaard -

In order to write about life first you must live it.

– Ernest Hemingway -

You never really learn much from hearing yourself speak.

– George Clooney -

Curiosity about life in all of its aspects, I think, is still the secret of great creative people.

– Leo Burnett -

Life imposes things on you that you can't control, but you still have the choice of how you're going to live through this.

– Celine Dion -

The way I see it, if you want the rainbow, you have to put up with the rain.

– Dolly Parton -

The unexamined life is not worth living.

– Socrates -

Don't settle for what life gives you; make life better and build something.

– Ashton Kutcher -

I like criticism. It makes you strong.

– LeBron James -

Everybody wants to be famous, but nobody wants to do the work. I live by that. You grind hard so you can play hard. At the end of the day, you put all the work in, and eventually it'll pay off. It could be in a year; it could be in 30 years. Eventually, your hard work will pay off.

– Kevin Hart -

My mama always said, life is like a box of chocolates. You never know what you're going to get.

– Forrest Gump (Forrest Gump Quotes) -

The healthiest response to life is joy.

– Deepak Chopra -

Everything negative – pressure, challenges – is all an opportunity for me to rise.

– Kobe Bryant -

Live for each second without hesitation.

– Elton John -

When I was 5 years old, my mother always told me that happiness was the key to life. When I went to school, they asked me what I wanted to be when I grew up. I wrote down 'happy'. They told me I didn't understand the assignment, and I told them they didn't understand life.

– John Lennon -

Life is never easy. There is work to be done and obligations to be met – obligations to truth, to justice, and to liberty.

– John F. Kennedy (JFK Quotes) -

Keep calm and carry on.

– Winston Churchill -

Life is like riding a bicycle. To keep your balance, you must keep moving.

– Albert Einstein -

Your work is going to fill a large part of your life, and the only way to be truly satisfied is to do what you believe is great work. And the only way to do great work is to love what you do. If you haven't found it yet, keep looking. Don't settle. As with all matters of the heart, you'll know when you find it.

– Steve Jobs -

Life is a succession of lessons which must be lived to be understood."

– Helen Keller -

Watch your thoughts; they become words. Watch your words; they become actions. Watch your actions; they become habits. Watch your habits; they become character. Watch your character; it becomes your destiny.

– Lao-Tze -

Life is really simple, but men insist on making it complicated.

– Confucius -

I just want you to know that if you are out there and you are being really hard on yourself right now for something that has happened... it's normal. That is what is going to happen to you in life. No one gets through unscathed. We are all going to have a few scratches on us. Please be kind to yourselves and stand up for yourself, please.

– Taylor Swift -

When we do the best we can, we never know what miracle is wrought in our life or the life of another.

– Helen Keller -

I've missed more than 9000 shots in my career. I've lost almost 300 games. 26 times I've been trusted to take the game winning shot and missed. I've failed over and over and over again in my life. And that is why I succeed...

– Michael Jordan -

Life is like a coin. You can spend it any way you wish, but you only spend it once.

– Lillian Dickson -

The best portion of a good man's life is his little nameless, unencumbered acts of kindness and of love.

– Wordsworth -

In three words I can sum up everything I've learned about life: It goes on.

– Robert Frost -

Life is ten percent what happens to you and ninety percent how you respond to it.

– Charles Swindoll -

The two most important days in your life are the day you are born and the day you find out why.

- Mark Twain -

Keep smiling, because life is a beautiful thing and there's so much to smile about.

– Marilyn Monroe -

You have brains in your head. You have feet in your shoes. You can steer yourself any direction you choose.

– Dr. Seuss -

Good friends, good books, and a sleepy conscience: this is the ideal life.

– Mark Twain -

Maybe that's what life is... a wink of the eye and winking stars.

– Jack Kerouac -

If you live long enough, you'll make mistakes. But if you learn from them, you'll be a better person.

– Bill Clinton -

Life is a flower of which love is the honey.

– Victor Hugo -

Life would be tragic if it weren't funny...

– Stephen Hawking -

Health is the greatest gift, contentment the greatest wealth, faithfulness the best relationship.

– Buddha -

If you spend your whole life waiting for the storm, you'll never enjoy the sunshine.

– Morris West -

Life's tragedy is that we get old too soon and wise too late.

— Benjamin Franklin -

he greatest pleasure of life is love.

– Euripides -

Live in the sunshine, swim the sea, drink the wild air.

– Ralph Waldo Emerson -

Too many of us are not living our dreams because we are living our fears.

– Les Brown -

I believe every human has a finite number of heartbeats. I don't intend to waste any of mine.

– Neil Armstrong -

Life is about making an impact, not making an income.

– Kevin Kruse -

Be courageous. Challenge orthodoxy. Stand up for what you believe in. When you are in your rocking chair talking to your grandchildren many years from now, be sure you have a good story to tell.

– Amal Clooney -

Every strike brings me closer to the next home run.

– Babe Ruth -

Life is what we make it, always has been, always will be.

– Grandma Moses -

When you cease to dream you cease to live.

– Malcolm Forbes -

There are no mistakes, only opportunities.

– Tina Fey -

If you're not stubborn, you'll give up on experiments too soon. And if you're not flexible, you'll pound your head against the wall and you won't see a different solution to a problem you're trying to solve.

– Jeff Bezos -

Life shrinks or expands in proportion to one's courage.

– Anais Nin -

Life is short, and it is here to be lived.

– Kate Winslet -

The longer I live, the more beautiful life becomes.

– Frank Lloyd Wright -

Every moment is a fresh beginning.

– T.S. Eliot -

Don't limit yourself. Many people limit themselves to what they think they can do. You can go as far as your mind lets you. What you believe, remember, you can achieve.

– Mary Kay Ash -

Live as if you were to die tomorrow. Learn as if you were to live forever.

– Mahatma Gandhi -

Don't cry because it's over, smile because it happened.

– Dr. Seuss -

If you can do what you do best and be happy, you're further along in life than most people.

– Leonardo DiCaprio -

We should remember that just as a positive outlook on life can promote good health, so can everyday acts of kindness.

– Hillary Clinton -

Identity is a prison you can never escape, but the way to redeem your past is not to run from it, but to try to understand it, and use it as a foundation to grow.

– Jay-Z -

It is our choices that show what we truly are, far more than our abilities.

– J. K. Rowling -

The best way to predict your future is to create it.

– Abraham Lincoln -

You must expect great things of yourself before you can do them.

– Michael Jordan -

It takes 20 years to build a reputation and five minutes to ruin it. If you think about that, you'll do things differently.

– Warren Buffett -

As you grow older, you will discover that you have two hands, one for helping yourself, the other for helping others.

– Audrey Hepburn -

It had long since come to my attention that people of accomplishment rarely sat back and let things happen to them. They went out and happened to things.

– Leonardo Da Vinci -

Sometimes you can't see yourself clearly until you see yourself through the eyes of others.

– Ellen DeGeneres -

I have learned to seek my happiness by limiting my desires, rather than in attempting to satisfy them.

– John Stuart Mill -

Nothing is more honorable than a grateful heart.

– Seneca -

You must not lose faith in humanity. Humanity is an ocean; if a few drops of the ocean are dirty, the ocean does not become dirty.

– Mahatma Gandhi -

When one door closes, another opens; but we often look so long and so regretfully upon the closed door that we do not see the one that has opened for us.

– Alexander Graham Bell -

All life is an experiment. The more experiments you make, the better.

– Ralph Waldo Emerson -

Happiness is the feeling that power increases — that resistance is being overcome.

– Friedrich Nietzsche -

Never take life seriously. Nobody gets out alive anyway.

– Anonymous -

Throughout life people will make you mad, disrespect you and treat you bad. Let God deal with the things they do, cause hate in your heart will consume you too.

– Will Smith -

It's never too late – never too late to start over, never too late to be happy.

– Jane Fonda -

Do not dwell in the past, do not dream of the future, concentrate the mind on the present moment.

– Buddha -

Life is a dream for the wise, a game for the fool, a comedy for the rich, a tragedy for the poor.

– Sholom Aleichem -

If you love life, don't waste time, for time is what life is made up of.

– Bruce Lee -

The greatest blessings of mankind are within us and within our reach. A wise man is content with his lot, whatever it may be, without wishing for what he has not.

– Seneca -

The secret of happiness, you see is not found in seeking more, but in developing the capacity to enjoy less.

– Socrates -

The more man mediates upon good thoughts, the better will be his world and the world at large.

– Confucius -

Be nice to people on the way up, because you may meet them on the way down.

– Jimmy Durante -

Be happy for this moment. This moment is your life.

– Omar Khayyam -

Don't be afraid to fail. It's not the end of the world, and in many ways, it's the first step toward learning something and getting better at it.

– Jon Hamm -

We become not a melting pot but a beautiful mosaic. Different people, different beliefs, different yearnings, different hopes, different dreams.

– Jimmy Carter -

Life is very interesting... in the end, some of your greatest pains, become your greatest strengths.

– Drew Barrymore -

I think if you live in a black-and-white world, you're going to suffer a lot. I used to be like that. But I don't believe that anymore.

– Bradley Cooper -

The minute that you're not learning I believe you're dead.

– Jack Nicholson -

There may be people who have more talent than you, but there's no excuse for anyone to work harder than you do – and I believe that.

– Derek Jeter -

Happiness is like a butterfly; the more you chase it, the more it will elude you, but if you turn your attention to other things, it will come and sit softly on your shoulder.

– Henry David Thoreau -

When it is obvious that goals can't be reached, don't adjust the goals, but adjust the action steps.

– Confucius -

You're not defined by your past; you're prepared by it. You're stronger, more experienced, and you have greater confidence.

– Joel Osteen -

Life's tough, but it's tougher when you're stupid.

– John Wayne -

I don't believe in happy endings, but I do believe in happy travels, because ultimately, you die at a very young age, or you live long enough to watch your friends die. It's a mean thing, life.

– George Clooney -

You're only human. You live once and life is wonderful, so eat the damned red velvet cupcake.

– Emma Stone -

A lot of people give up just before they're about to make it. You know you never know when that next obstacle is going to be the last one.

– Chuck Norris (related: 101 Chuck Norris Jokes) -

I guess it comes down to a simple choice, really. Get busy living or get busy dying.

– «Shawshank Redemption» -

Find people who will make you better.

– Michelle Obama -

I believe you make your day. You make your life. So much of it is all perception, and this is the form that I built for myself. I have to accept it and work within those compounds, and it's up to me.

– Brad Pitt -

When we strive to become better than we are, everything around us becomes better too.

– Paulo Coelho -

Don't allow your past or present condition to control you. It's just a process that you're going through to get you to the next level.

– T.D. Jakes -

You only pass through this life once, you don't come back for an encore.

– Elvis Presley -

Make each day your masterpiece.

– John Wooden -

Take up one idea. Make that one idea your life — think of it, dream of it, live on that idea. Let the brain, muscles, nerves, every part of your body be full of that idea, and just leave every other idea alone. This is the way to success.

– Swami Vivekananda -

The more you praise and celebrate your life, the more there is in life to celebrate.

– Oprah Winfrey -

As my knowledge of things grew, I felt more and more the delight of the world I was in.

– Helen Keller -

Be where you are; otherwise, you will miss your life.

– Buddha -

And that is how change happens. One gesture. One person. One moment at a time.

– Libba Bray, The Sweet Far Thing -

There are three things you can do with your life: You can waste it, you can spend it, or you can invest it. The best use of your life is to invest it in something that will last longer than your time on Earth.

– Rick Warren -

In the long run, the sharpest weapon of all is a kind and gentle spirit.

– Anne Frank -

Once you figure out who you are and what you love about yourself, I think it all kinda falls into place.

– Jennifer Aniston -

Happy is the man who can make a living by his hobby.

– George Bernard Shaw -

Just disconnect. Once in a day sometime, sit silently and from all connections disconnect yourself.

– Yoda (Star Wars Quotes) -

Living an experience, a particular fate, is accepting it fully.

– Albert Camus -

Nobody who ever gave his best regretted it.

– George Halas -

Your image isn't your character. Character is what you are as a person.

– Derek Jeter -

Football is like life, it requires perseverance, self-denial, hard work sacrifice, dedication and respect for authority.

– Vince Lombardi -

Life isn't about waiting for the storm to pass; it's about learning to dance in the rain.

– Vivian Greene -

As you know, life is an echo; we get what we give.

– David DeNotaris -

There are no regrets in life, just lessons.

– Jennifer Aniston -

I believe that nothing in life is unimportant every moment can be a beginning.

– John McLeod -

You choose the life you live. If you don't like it, it's on you to change it because no one else is going to do it for you.

– Kim Kiyosaki -

If we don't change, we don't grow. If we don't grow, we aren't really living.

– Gail Sheehy -

Benjamin Franklin was a humanitarian that dedicated his life to making contributions to all humans. He had a clear purpose for himself: improve the human race.

– Paulo Braga -

You cannot control everything that happens to you; you can only control the way you respond to what happens. In your response is your power.

– Anonymous -

You will meet two kinds of people in life: ones who build you up and ones who tear you down. But in the end, you'll thank them both.

– Anonymous -

I enjoy life when things are happening. I don't care if it's good things or bad things. That means you're alive.

– Joan Rivers -

Today, you have 100% of your life left.

– Tom Landry (Football Quotes) -

My mission in life is not merely to survive, but to thrive; and to do so with some passion, some compassion, some humor, and some style.

– Maya Angelou -

There's more to life than basketball. The most important thing is your family and taking care of each other and loving each other no matter what.

– Stephen Curry -

You never change things by fighting the existing reality. To change something, build a new model that makes the existing model obsolete.

– Buckminster Fuller -

You can't put a limit on anything. The more you dream, the farther you get.

– Michael Phelps -

Change, like healing, takes time.

– Veronica Roth -

Life doesn't require that we be the best, only that we try our best.

– H. Jackson Brown Jr. -

The way I see it, every life is a pile of good things and bad things. The good things don't always soften the bad things, but vice versa, the bad things don't always spoil the good things and make them unimportant.

– Doctor Who -

Change will not come if we wait for some other person, or if we wait for some other time. We are the ones we've been waiting for. We are the change that we seek.

– Barack Obama -

When you arise in the morning, think of what a precious privilege it is to be alive, to breathe, to think, to enjoy, to love.

– Marcus Aurelius -

Write it on your heart that every day is the best day in the year.

– Ralph Waldo Emerson -

Believe something and the Universe is on its way to being changed. Because you've changed, by believing. Once you've changed, other things start to follow. Isn't that the way it works?

– Diane Duane -

It is impossible to live without failing at something, unless you live so cautiously, that you might as well not have lived at all – in which case you fail by default.

– Anonymous -

It find the best way to love someone is not to change them, but instead, help them reveal the greatest version of themselves.

– Steve Maraboli

If I am not for myself, who will be for me? But if I am only for myself, what am I? And if not now, when?

– *Hillel* -

I alone cannot change the world, but I can cast a stone across the waters to create many ripples.

– *Mother Teresa* -

To change one's life: 1. Start immediately. 2. Do it flamboyantly. 3. No exceptions.

– *William James* -

Incredible change happens in your life when you decide to take control of what you do have power over instead of craving control over what you don't.

– *Steve Maraboli* -

Fashion changes, but style endures.

– *Coco Chanel* -

Some people dream of success, while other people get up every morning and make it happen.

– Wayne Huizenga -

The world as we have created it is a process of our thinking. It cannot be changed without changing our thinking.

– Albert Einstein -

Things change. And friends leave. Life doesn't stop for anybody.

– Stephen Chbosky -

I have accepted fear as part of life – specifically the fear of change... I have gone ahead despite the pounding in the heart that says: turn back...

– Erica Jong -

You cannot change what you are, only what you do.

– Philip Pullman -

Yesterday I was clever, so I wanted to change the world. Today I am wise, so I am changing myself.

– Rumi -

I don't need a friend who changes when I change and who nods when I nod; my shadow does that much better.

– Plutarch -

Nothing is so painful to the human mind as a great and sudden change.

– Mary Shelley -

Life is a series of natural and spontaneous changes. Don't resist them; that only creates sorrow. Let reality be reality. Let things flow naturally forward in whatever way they like.

– Lao Tzu -

Time takes it all, whether you want it to or not.

– Stephen King, The Green Mile -

Maturity is when you stop complaining and making excuses, and start making changes.

– Roy T. Bennett -

The philosophers have only interpreted the world, in various ways. The point, however, is to change it.

– Karl Marx -

Change the way you look at things and the things you look at change.

– Wayne W. Dyer -

We are not trapped or locked up in these bones. No, no. We are free to change. And love changes us. And if we can love one another, we can break open the sky.

– Walter Mosley -

To improve is to change; to be perfect is to change often.

– Winston S. Churchill -

Some changes look negative on the surface but you will soon realize that space is being created in your life for something new to emerge.

– Eckhart Tolle -

Taking a new step, uttering a new word, is what people fear most.

– Fyodor Dostoevsky, « Crime and Punishment» -

Every woman that finally figured out her worth, has picked up her suitcases of pride and boarded a flight to freedom, which landed in the valley of change.

– Shannon L. Alder -

You're always you, and that don't change, and you're always changing, and there's nothing you can do about it.

– Neil Gaiman, The Graveyard Book -

Change begins at the end of your comfort zone.

– Roy T. Bennett -

No matter who you are, no matter what you did, no matter where you've come from, you can always change, become a better version of yourself.

— Madonna -

Anger, resentment and jealousy doesn't change the heart of others— it only changes yours.

— Shannon Alder -

Faced with the choice between changing one's mind and proving that there is no need to do so, almost everyone gets busy on the proof.

— John Kenneth Galbraith -

When you come out of the storm, you won't be the same person who walked in. That's what this storm's all about.

— Haruki Murakami -

True life is lived when tiny changes occur.

— Leo Tolstoy -

When people are ready to, they change. They never do it before then, and sometimes they die before they get around to it. You can't make them change if they don't want to, just like when they do want to, you can't stop them.

– Andy Warhol -

One child, one teacher, one book, one pen can change the world.

– Malala Yousafzai -

If you're in a bad situation, don't worry it'll change. If you're in a good situation, don't worry it'll change.

– John A. Simone, Sr. -

Everyone has highs and lows that they have to learn from, but every morning I start off with a good head on my shoulders, saying to myself, 'It's going to be a good day!"

– Lindsay Lohan -

Every hundred feet the world changes.

– Roberto Bolaño -

No one can tell what goes on in between the person you were and the person you become. No one can chart that blue and lonely section of hell. There are no maps of the change. You just come out the other side. Or you don't.

– Stephen King, The Stand -

Vulnerability is the birthplace of innovation, creativity and change.

– Brene Brown -

People are very open-minded about new things, as long as they're exactly like the old ones.

– Charles F. Kettering -

Desperation is the raw material of drastic change. Only those who can leave behind everything they have ever believed in can hope to escape.

– William S. Burroughs -

Nothing endures but change.

– Heraclitus -

The people who are crazy enough to think they can change the world are the ones who do.

– Steve Jobs -

I give you this to take with you: Nothing remains as it was. If you know this, you can begin again, with pure joy in the uprooting.

– Judith Minty -

A bend in the road is not the end of the road... Unless you fail to make the turn.

– Helen Keller -

Morning comes whether you set the alarm or not.

– Ursula K. Le Guin -

Life belongs to the living, and he who lives must be prepared for changes.

– Johann Wolfgang von Goethe -

Change may not always bring growth, but there is no growth without change.

– Roy T. Bennett -

I remind myself every morning: Nothing I say this day will teach me anything. So, if I'm going to learn, I must do it by listening.

– Larry King -

Anyone who isn't embarrassed of who they were last year probably isn't learning enough.

– Alain de Botton -

Change is the end result of all true learning.

– Leo Buscaglia -

Our ability to adapt is amazing. Our ability to change isn't quite as spectacular.

– Lisa Lutz -

It's not that some people have willpower and some don't...
It's that some people are ready to change and others are
not.

— James Gordon -

Changing is what people do when they have no options left.

— Holly Black -

Now that your eyes are open, make the sun jealous with
your burning passion to start the day. Make the sun jealous
or stay in bed.

— Malak El Halabi -

To change ourselves effectively, we first had to change our
perceptions.

— Stephen R. Covey -

Nothing is lost...Everything is transformed.

— Michael Ende -

Every morning was a cheerful invitation to make my life of equal simplicity, and I may say innocence, with Nature herself.

– Henry David Thoreau -

The changes we dread most may contain our salvation.

– Barbara Kingsolver -

The past can teach us, nurture us, but it cannot sustain us. The essence of life is change, and we must move ever forward or the soul will wither and die.

– Susanna Kearsley -

If you want to change attitudes, start with a change in behavior.

– Katherine Hepburn -

If you want to make enemies, try to change something.

– Woodrow Wilson -

You tried to change, didn't you? Closed your mouth more, tried to be softer, prettier, less volatile, less awake... You can't make homes out of human beings. Someone should have already told you that.

– Warsan Shire -

Don't knock the weather; nine-tenths of the people couldn't start a conversation if it didn't change once in a while.

– Kin Hubbard -

Change your thoughts and you change your world.

– Norman Vincent Peale -

In these times you have to be an optimist to open your eyes when you awake in the morning.

– Carl Sandburg -

We first make our habits, then our habits make us.

– John Dryden -

You make a choice: continue living your life feeling muddled in this abyss of self-misunderstanding, or you find your identity independent of it. You draw your own box.

−Duchess Meghan -

Change your life today. Don't gamble on the future, act now, without delay.

− Simone de Beauvoir -

he great growling engine of change − technology.

− Alvin Toffler -

The only difference between a rut and a grave is their dimensions.

− Ellen Glasgow -

Folks, I don't trust children. They're here to replace us.

− Stephen Colbert -

No matter what people will tell you, words and ideas can change the world.

– Robin Williams -

People change for two reasons; either they learned a lot or they've been hurt too much.

– Unknown -

The secret of change is to focus all of your energy, not on fighting the old, but on building the new.

– Socrates -

Act the way you'd like to be and soon you'll be the way you'd like to act.

– Bob Dylan -

Change is hardest at the beginning, messiest in the middle and best at the end.

– Robin Sharma -

And all the lives we ever lived and all the lives to be are full of trees and changing leaves.

– Virginia Woolf «To the Lighthouse» -

People who can change and change again are so much more reliable and happier than those who can't.

– Stephen Fry -

What people have the capacity to choose, they have the ability to change.

– Madeleine Albright -

If we don't change, we don't grow. If we don't grow, we aren't really living.

– Anatole France -

It was long since I had longed for anything and the effect on me was horrible.

– Samuel Beckett -

I want to be in the arena. I want to be brave with my life. And when we make the choice to dare greatly, we sign up to get our asses kicked. We can choose courage or we can choose comfort, but we can't have both. Not at the same time.

– Brene Brown -

People can cry much easier than they can change.

– James Baldwin -

Change almost never fails because it's too early. It almost always fails because it's too late.

– Seth Godin -

I wanted change and excitement and to shoot off in all directions myself, like the colored arrows from a Fourth of July rocket.

– Sylvia Plath -

All is flux, nothing stays still.

– Plato -

People tell you the world looks a certain way. Parents tell you how to think. Schools tell you how to think. TV. Religion. And then at a certain point, if you're lucky, you realize you can make up your own mind. Nobody sets the rules but you. You can design your own life.

— Carrie Ann Moss -

Words are where most change begins.

— Brandon Sanderson -

People don't change, they just have momentary steps outside of their true character.

— Chad Kultgen -

Consider how hard it is to change yourself and you'll understand what little chance you have in trying to change others.

— Jacob M. Braude -

Bending beats breaking.

— Betty Greene -

Either way, change will come. It could be bloody, or it could be beautiful. It depends on us.

– Arundhati Roy -

What is necessary to change a person is to change his awareness of himself.

– Abraham Maslow -

Sometimes you hit a point where you either change or self-destruct.

– Sam Stevens -

People don't resist change. They resist being changed.

– Peter Senge -

The greatest discovery of all time is that a person can change his future by merely changing his attitude.

– Oprah Winfrey -

We change the world not by what we say or do, but as a consequence of what we have become.

– Dr. David Hawkins -

The struggles we endure today will be the 'good old days' we laugh about tomorrow.

– Aaron Lauritsen -

The world doesn't change in front of your eyes, it changes behind your back.

– Terry Hayes -

There is nothing impossible to they who will try.

– Alexander the Great -

Man cannot remake himself without suffering, for he is both the marble and the sculptor.

– Alexis Carrel -

If you make your internal life a priority, then everything else you need on the outside will be given to you and it will be extremely clear what the next step is.

– Gabrielle Bernstein -

When you have a dream, you've got to grab it and never let go.

– Carol Burnett -

Keep your face always toward the sunshine, and shadows will fall behind you.

– Walt Whitman -

Nothing is impossible. The word itself says 'I'm possible!

– Audrey Hepburn -

Do not allow people to dim your shine because they are blinded. Tell them to put some sunglasses on.

– Lady Gaga -

At the end of the day, whether or not those people are comfortable with how you're living your life doesn't matter. What matters is whether you're comfortable with it.

– Dr. Phil -

The bad news is time flies. The good news is you're the pilot.

– Michael Altshuler -

Life has got all those twists and turns. You've got to hold on tight and off you go.

– Nicole Kidman -

In a gentle way, you can shake the world.

– Mahatma Gandhi -

You don't always need a plan. Sometimes you just need to breathe, trust, let go and see what happens.

– Mandy Hale -

For me, becoming isn't about arriving somewhere or achieving a certain aim. I see it instead as forward motion, a means of evolving, a way to reach continuously toward a better self. The journey doesn't end.

– Michelle Obama -

Success is not final; failure is not fatal: it is the courage to continue that counts.

– Winston Churchill -

You define your own life. Don't let other people write your script.

– Oprah Winfrey -

You are never too old to set another goal or to dream a new dream.

– Malala Yousafzai -

Spread love everywhere you go.

– Mother Teresa -

Everyone has inside of him a piece of good news. The good news is that you don't know how great you can be! How much you can love! What you can accomplish! And what your potential is!

– Anne Frank -

It is during our darkest moments that we must focus to see the light.

– Aristotle -

You can be everything. You can be the infinite amount of things that people are.

– Kesha -

Not having the best situation, but seeing the best in your situation is the key to happiness.

– Marie Forleo -

Tides do what tides do—they turn.

– Derek Landy -

You gain strength, courage, and confidence by every experience in which you really stop to look fear in the face. You are able to say to yourself, 'I lived through this horror. I can take the next thing that comes along.' You must do the thing you think you cannot do.

– Eleanor Roosevelt -

What lies behind you and what lies in front of you, pales in comparison to what lies inside of you.

– Ralph Waldo Emerson -

I'm not going to continue knocking that old door that doesn't open for me. I'm going to create my own door and walk through that.

– Ava DuVernay -

When it comes to luck, you make your own.

– Bruce Springsteen -

Nobody built like you, you design yourself.

– Jay-Z -

I'm going to be gone one day, and I have to accept that tomorrow isn't promised. Am I OK with how I'm living today? It's the only thing I can help. If I didn't have another one, what have I done with all my todays? Am I doing a good job?

– Hayley Williams -

Learning how to be still, to really be still and let life happen—that stillness becomes a radiance.

– Morgan Freeman -

No matter what people tell you, words and ideas can change the world.

– Robin Williams
as John Keating In Dead Poets Society -

Believe you can and you're halfway there.

– Theodore Roosevelt -

Belief creates the actual fact.

– William James -

Weaknesses are just strengths in the wrong environment.
– Marianne Cantwell -

Just don't give up trying to do what you really want to do. Where there is love and inspiration, I don't think you can go wrong.
– Ella Fitzgerald -

Silence is the last thing the world will ever hear from me.
– Marlee Matlin -

If you have good thoughts they will shine out of your face like sunbeams and you will always look lovely.
– Roald Dahl -

Treat everyone with politeness and kindness, not because they are nice, but because you are.
– Roy T. Bennett, The Light in the Heart -

Real change, enduring change, happens one step at a time.
– Ruth Bader Ginsburg -

Find out who you are and be that person. That's what your soul was put on this earth to be. Find that truth, live that truth, and everything else will come.
– Ellen DeGeneres -

Wake up determined, go to bed satisfied.
– Dwayne "The Rock" Johnson -

All you need is the plan, the road map, and the courage to press on to your destination.
– Earl Nightingale -

I have learned over the years that when one's mind is made up, this diminishes fear; knowing what must be done does away with fear.
– Rosa Parks -

I tell myself, 'You've been through so much, you've endured so much, time will allow me to heal, and soon this will be just another memory that made me the strong woman, athlete, and mother I am today.

– Serena Williams -

I care about decency and humanity and kindness. Kindness today is an act of rebellion

– Pink -

We must let go of the life we have planned, so as to accept the one that is waiting for us.

– Joseph Campbell -

There's nothing more powerful than not giving a f—k.

– Amy Schumer -

Faith is love taking the form of aspiration.

– William Ellery Channing -

Our lives are stories in which we write, direct and star in the leading role. Some chapters are happy while others bring lessons to learn, but we always have the power to be the heroes of our own adventures.

– Joelle Speranza -

Life is like riding a bicycle. To keep your balance, you must keep moving.

– Albert Einstein -

Don't try to lessen yourself for the world; let the world catch up to you.

– Beyoncé -

Live your beliefs and you can turn the world around.

– Henry David Thoreau -

We are not our best intentions. We are what we do.

– Amy Dickinson -

When you've seen beyond yourself, then you may find, peace of mind is waiting there.

– George Harrison -

I've noticed when I fear something, if I just end up doing it, I'm grateful in the end.

– Colleen Hoover -

We generate fears while we sit. We overcome them by action.

– Dr. Henry Link -

We need to take risks. We need to go broke. We need to prove them wrong, simply by not giving up.

– Awkwafina -

I believe that if you'll just stand up and go, life will open up for you. Something just motivates you to keep moving.

– Tina Turner -

What you get by achieving your goals is not as important as what you become by achieving your goals.

– Zig Ziglar -

If you don't like the road you're walking, start paving another one!

– Dolly Parton -

You are never too old to set another goal or to dream a new dream.

– C.S. Lewis -

I'm realizing how much I've diminished my own power. I'm not doing that no more.

– Alicia Keys -

The simple act of listening to someone and making them feel as if they have truly been heard is a most treasured gift.

– L. A. Villafane -

Dreams don't have to just be dreams. You can make it a reality; if you just keep pushing and keep trying, then eventually you'll reach your goal. And if that takes a few years, then that's great, but if it takes 10 or 20, then that's part of the process.

– Naomi Osaka -

When we let fear be our master, we cannot be happy and free as a butterfly. But when we choose to trust the journey and embrace love and joy, we are free to fly.

– Annicken R. Day -

Work hard, know your s—t, show your s—t, and then feel entitled.

– Mindy Kaling -

Out of the mountain of despair, a stone of hope.

– Martin Luther King, Jr. -

I like to believe that you don't need to reach a certain goal to be happy. I prefer to think that happiness is always there, and that when things don't go the way we might like them to, it's a sign from above that something even better is right around the corner.

— *David Archuleta* -

We've been making our own opportunities, and as you prove your worth and value to people, they can't put you in a box. You hustle it into happening, right?

— *Jennifer Lopez* -

We all have problems. But it's not what happens to us, [it's] the choices we make after.

— *Elizabeth Smart* -

It is never too late to be what you might have been.

— *George Eliot* -

We have to be better. We have to love more, hate less. We have to listen more and talk less. We have to know that this is everybody's responsibility.

– Meghan Rapinoe -

How wild it was, to let it be.

– Cheryl Strayed -

You have to be where you are to get where you need to go.

– Amy Poehler -

Whatever you think the world is withholding from you, you are withholding from the world.

– Eckhart Tolle -

Don't be afraid. Because you're going to be afraid. But remember when you become afraid, just don't be afraid.

– Joan Jett -

You don't have to be defined or confined by your environment, by your family circumstances, and certainly not by your race or gender.

– Mariah Carey -

Let love rule.

– Lenny Kravitz -

You do not find the happy life. You make it.

– Camilla Eyring Kimball -

The only limit to our realization of tomorrow will be our doubts today.

– Franklin Delano Roosevelt -

Perfection is not attainable, but if we chase perfection, we can catch excellence.

– Vince Lombardi -

Definitions belong to the definers, not the defined.

– Toni Morrison -

You must find the place inside yourself where nothing is impossible.

– Deepak Chopra -

In order for the light to shine so brightly, the darkness must be present.

– Sir Francis Bacon -

It ain't about how hard you hit. It's about how hard you can get hit and keep moving forward.

– Sylvester Stallone in Rocky Balboa -

Trying to grow up is hurting. You make mistakes. You try to learn from them, and when you don't, it hurts even more.

– Aretha Franklin -

Being vulnerable is a strength, not a weakness.

– Selena Gomez -

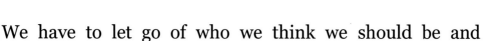

We have to let go of who we think we should be and embrace what is.

– Achea Redd -

A lot of people are afraid to say what they want. That's why they don't get what they want.

– Madonna -

I don't look ahead. I'm right here with you. It's a good way to be.

– Danny DeVito -

Clouds come floating into my life, no longer to carry rain or usher storm, but to add color to my sunset sky.

– Rabindranath Tagore -

The only journey is the one within.

– Rainer Maria Rilke -

Great goals make great people. People cannot hit what they do not aim for.

- Roy T. Bennett -

I will not let anyone scare me out of my full potential.

– Nicki Minaj -

Wisdom comes from experience. Experience is often a result of lack of wisdom.

– Terry Pratchett -

Never bend your head. Always hold it high. Look the world straight in the eye.

– Helen Keller -

The power of imagination makes us infinite.

– John Muir -

If my mind can conceive it, if my heart can believe it, then I can achieve it.

– Muhammad Ali -

Embrace the glorious mess that you are.

– Elizabeth Gilbert -

When someone loves you, the way they talk about you is different. You feel safe and comfortable.

– Jess C. Scott, The Intern -

To live is the rarest thing in the world. Most people exist, that is all.

– Oscar Wilde -

The moral of my story is the sun always comes out after the storm. Being optimistic and surrounding yourself with positive loving people is for me, living life on the sunny side of the street.

– Janice Dean -

The only way out of the labyrinth of suffering is to forgive.

– John Green,
Looking for Alaska -

I'm the one that's got to die when it's time for me to die, so let me live my life the way I want to.

– Jimi Hendrix -

You yourself, as much as anybody in the entire universe, deserve your love and affection.

– Sharon Salzburg -

I am experienced enough to do this. I am knowledgeable enough to do this. I am prepared enough to do this. I am mature enough to do this. I am brave enough to do this.

– Alexandria Ocasio-Cortez
In Knock Down The House -

Here's to the crazy ones, the misfits, the rebels, the troublemakers, the round pegs in the square holes... the ones who see things differently — they're not fond of rules... You can quote them, disagree with them, glorify or vilify them, but the only thing you can't do is ignore them because they change things... They push the human race forward, and while some may see them as the crazy ones, we see genius...

– Steve Jobs -

This life is what you make it. No matter what, you're going to mess up sometimes, it's a universal truth. But the good part is you get to decide how you're going to mess it up. Girls will be your friends - they'll act like it anyway. But remember, some come, some go. The ones that stay with you through everything - they're your true best friends. Don't let go of them. Also remember, sisters, make the best friends in the world. As for lovers, well, they'll come and go too. And baby, I hate to say it, most of them - actually pretty much all of them are going to break your heart, but you can't give up because if you give up, you'll never find your soulmate. You'll never find that half who makes you whole, and that goes for everything. Just because you fail once, doesn't mean you're going to fail at everything. Keep trying, hold on, and always, always, always believe in yourself, because if you don't, then who will, sweetie? Keep your head high, keep your chin up, and most importantly, keep smiling, because life's a beautiful thing and there's so much to smile about.

– Marilyn Monroe -

Allow these 365 inspirational quotes about life fill your day to day give an extra boost when you may need it. Store them on your phone or computer to read whenever you need it!

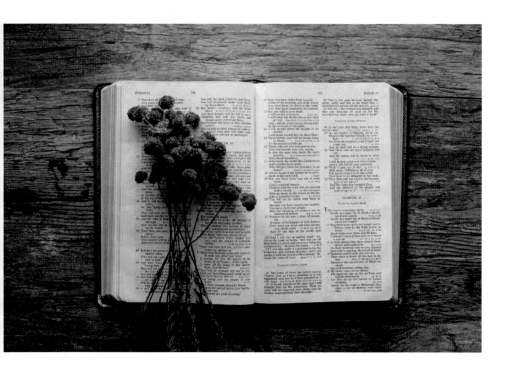

LIFE IS A GREAT GIFT!

Notes

_____

_____

_____

_____

_____

_____

_____

_____

_____

_____

_____

_____

_____

_____

_____

_____

_____

_____

_____

_____

_____

_____

_____

_____

_____

Made in the USA
Las Vegas, NV
30 September 2021

31462678R00055